MARIA ROSE SOTELO

Recovery

Releasing the pain of breaking down by pretending to be a poet.

Copyright © 2022 by Maria Rose Sotelo

All rights reserved. No part of this publication may be reproduced, stored or transmitted in any form or by any means, electronic, mechanical, photocopying, recording, scanning, or otherwise without written permission from the publisher. It is illegal to copy this book, post it to a website, or distribute it by any other means without permission.

First edition

This book was professionally typeset on Reedsy.
Find out more at reedsy.com

To the friends who stand by me both crazy and sane.
To the one who taught me if you go quietly through the trauma it is okay to heal loudly.
To the one who makes sure I am still pushing forward even when I want to stop.
To the one who picked up the slack I could not carry while lying on the ground.
I love and appreciate each of you more than you can ever know.

Contents

Preface   iv

I   Broken

Lost.	3
Falling.	5
Balance.	7
Run.	8
Fear.	9
Surrender.	10
Judgment.	12
Creator.	13
Limits.	14
Letting Go.	15
Breaking.	16
Bees.	17
Meditation.	18
Done.	19
Dark.	20
Remnant.	21
Blind.	22
Fighting.	23
Crumble.	24
Prayer.	25

Inches.   26

II   Healing

Nine.	29
Dam.	30
Shrouded.	32
Overstimulated Bedtime	33
Reset.	34
Feeling.	35
Oceans.	36
Tipping Scales.	37
Identity.	38
Busy.	39
Anger.	40
Failure.	41
Push.	42
Rest.	43
Hidden.	44
Confused.	45
Judging.	46
Roaming.	47
Cycle.	48
Release.	49
Staircase.	50
Aspirations.	52
So Close.	53
Forgiven.	54
Inches.	55
Dreams.	56
Inner Child.	57

III   Living.

Cyclothymia.	61
Re-Write	62
Masks.	63
Stop.	64
Pause.	65
Worthy.	66
Acceptance.	67

Preface

Thirty-four years. The exact amount of time I enjoyed life before having confirmed what I long suspected…. there are a few glitches in the programming of my brain. Sadly, this was only discovered through breaking down. Warning signs were overlooked, and sometimes blatantly ignored; and the end result was a lot of quality face time with my carpet, a partial hospitalization, and endless therapy and medication shifts before getting my brain and life back on the rails.

During the months of working to rebuild I found an outlet in journals a prose and assembled this collection of thoughts and emotions. Writing was became a way to release the toxins from my veins with words flowing out in place of blood.

I hope it speaks to you. I hope it reminds you that we are all going through battles. And I hope it brings you some measure of peace to know that even though we sometimes must crawl through the darkest of spaces they can lead us to healing and joy.

I

Broken

These words and feelings dripped from my soul as I approached the edge and faced my broken mind. Many are but half thoughts captured as they flew by while I worked to survive long enough to think again.

Lost.

How did I arrive at this place?
   I am not even sure who I am anymore.
   God I am sorry.

I…I just can't keep doing this.
   I can't look at myself in the mirror.
   I don't want to look at my life.

How did I get to this point?
   I tried so hard for so long.
   And then I just stopped.

How do I learn to feel again?
   Can I dig through the rubbish
   to find out what is left underneath?

I can't keep floating through this life
   Thoughtless
   Emotionless

Shallow.

To learn to breathe again I must dive
   Deep and head first.

Falling.

Why
   Is it
   The
   Only way
   I truly understand
   Just how high you brought me

Is by watching
   myself
   F
   A
   L
   L
   ?

What did it bring you?
   Why did you need to do it?
   What about hurting me brought you joy?
   Why didn't you keep walking past?

Recovery

It breaks my heart to think that you enjoyed watching the fall even as I shattered watching my hope crumble.

Balance.

Where is the middle ground?
   Why must one waiver between living on the verge of collapse and racing towards the edge?

How do you find yourself when waves of exhaustion are drowning out each sound?
   How can you put yourself first when so many other priorities are falling apart?
   Why is balance so impossible to find?

Is there even a way to have it all?
   Is there even a way to survive barely having it together at all?
   Does anyone else fantasize of running away and leaving it all behind?

Why can't we find balance so we can live, not just survive?

Run.

~~~

What are you avoiding?

Why do I always have to be busy?

What is the source of pain that we are running from?

Is there one cut or many pushing us to run from our own hearts and minds?

If we pause and lower our walls will we survive or be swept away by the pain the hides inside?

Fear.

Why do I fear failure,
   what even does it mean to fail?

Why do I feel like a failure
   even in the midst of my success?

Why does there always have to be more?
   Can't it be okay to just stay as I am?

Why must we strive to prove ourselves each day?
   Who are you proving yourself to?

Why can I not just be enough for myself and forget everyone else's voice?
   What would it take to love yourself
   to accept yourself…
   As you are, where you are, and with all you have accomplished?

Surrender.

It is okay not to be okay.
  Surrender can be a form of release.
  Learn to let go of your need to be everything and do everything
  Life is the longest thing you will ever do; don't ruin it with undo expectations.

No one else needs to define your success.
  It is okay to stop.
  It is okay to pause.
  It is okay to let go.

Stop building a guillotine of expectation above your head.
  Live your life without treating it like a to do list.
  Don't fill your plate so full that it makes you feel sick instead of satisfied.

Be okay with the idea of failure.
  Be okay with letting dreams go so that new ones can come.

Surrender.

Everyone fails.

Failure is not the end, but a new beginning.
You might even like yourself and your life better after you let yourself fail.

Judgment.

What would you say to your best friend, child, partner if they were in your shoes?

Would you judge them or support them?

Would you push them harder and only accept them if they meet your definition of success?

Or, would you hold them and love them and cherish them when they are falling?

Why are you holding yourself hostage to expectations you would place on no one else?

Let go.

Just stop.

Stop hurting your mind and body and soul with judgments and expectations you don't deserve.

Creator.

~~~~~

Sometimes when I begin creating I find myself filled with a burning need to make something better.

It becomes nearly an obsession to push my thoughts outside of myself.

I must go past what I have done before and create something bigger and better.

I find myself ill content until I have exceeded my own expectations and limits.

Was this how God, the original Creator, felt?

If so how beyond comprehension is it that we are the masterpiece after which He could rest?

Limits.

I **can** do all things does not mean I can do all of the things.
 I am a human.
 I have limits.
 And that is okay.

Letting Go.

Life wont always be what you expected it to be.
   Things change.

Embrace the reality of what is.
   Let go of what could have been.
   Move forward into what will be.

Breaking.

Have you ever wondered what it feels like to fall apart?
   It is a heady blend of fog, focus and pain.

Hours go by in the blink of an eye,
   But minutes last for days.

Sometimes you cannot feel your body.
   Other times every single nerve ending is on fire and you can feel sound.

Will I even remember any of this when I finally wake?

Bees.

Anxiety overwhelms my mind,
    Thoughts buzzing like bees.

They swoop and dive down,
    Landing only to sting the most tender recesses of my consciousness.

They swirl lower filling my chest with tension,
    Constricting my lungs and stealing my breath.

Their incessant presence removes my connection to reality,
    I slowly drown in my thoughts.

Meditation.

I breathe in,
    Focusing on my breath.

I follow the air as it fills my lungs and surrounds my heart.
    If only it would carry my heart along with it as I exhale.

Done.

Today I want to be done.

The appeal of the dark is so strong,
  Drawing me in,
  Calling my name.

To float.
  To feel the calm and cool embrace of unconsciousness as it lulls me into oblivion.

A couple of pills,
  A handful of shots,
  And hours and hours of blissful peace.

Dark.

I don't want to die,
  But I don't want to live my life.

I am smothered by the weight of my existence,
  Each moment another demand flows in and my mind cannot contain itself.

I open my seams and pour out my light to fulfill all you ask,
  Leaving me lost in the dark.

Remnant.

Breaking down feels like shutting down.
   Your soul folds in on itself,
   Attempting to protect the remnants of your identity that linger.

My brain is on fire,
   But my mind cannot lift its eyes to form a response to the pain.

I want to float away.
   I want to make it stop.

I need a break from being me.

Blind.

Where do you look when nowhere is safe?
  The past breaks my heart.
  The future is yet to be written.
  And in this moment I am falling apart.

Where do you focus when no time is safe?

Fighting.

Why do we compound our agony with guilt and shame?
   Isn't it bad enough to feel broken?

Isn't it enough to fight the demons and chemical imbalances plaguing our hearts and minds without having to fight our own self incrimination?

Crumble

What do you do when your life begins to crumble?

How do you fight when the enemy lives inside your broken mind?

There is no escape when you carry the attacker inside your chest and skull,
  consuming each thought and stealing each breath.

How do I stop the collapse when I myself am the cause?

Prayer.

Let me find rest in Your embrace.
   Let me accept what is and wait in the hope of Your love.
   Give me patience to hold onto You through my trials
   And allow Your joy to drown my doubts and fears.

Inches.

Only you have the power to push past your mental and emotional blocks.
   You can push.
   Inch by inch.
   Day by day.

                    You will move your way to the other side.

II

Healing

Coming through the collapse is only the beginning. The healing requires you dig out from the deep. The quagmire of pain and heartache that must be faced, must be purged. The burning feelings of acceptance and release allow you to move beyond your own pain and into the light of a new day.

Nine.

Nine pills.
   Nine little tablets to pacify my mind.
   Nine numbing buttons swallowed in succession,
   To make me capable of being in this moment and handling this space.

Seeing these faces,
   Smiling that I made the effort to come,
   Not worried one moment about the pain that I am in.

Nine little pills to dull the betrayal.
   Nine little pills to keep me from taking ninety more.

Dam.

The dam broke.
    The flood is sweeping me away.

For years I built it,
    Ever stronger.
    Each day pouring more cement.

For every burden another wall,
    My world inside growing smaller each day.

Then the weight grew,
    Cracking my walls.
    I plugged the small holes,
    Watching thin cracks expand inch by inch.

But today the dam broke.
    Your judgment a weight it could not bear.

Now I float midst the debris,

Dam.

Tumbling ever deeper through the dark inside of me.

Shrouded.

I can't tie the moments together anymore.
   A minute lasts an hour,
   An hour lasts a month,
   A month is but a second.

My notion of time is skewed
   By fragmented memories in my mind.

Some of the fragments slip through my fingers.
   Some fade from existence.

What remains I piece together,
   But they never quite align.

Will I remember these days?
   Or will their fragments be forever shrouded in gray?

Overstimulated Bedtime

Each door slams with the force of a hurricane
    Causing my muscles to tense to their snapping point.

Each word spoken,
    A scarab crawling through my skull with razor sharp feet,
    Stabbing as they go.

Why are my kids' rooms so far away?
    The journey will take until dawn.

I speak a prayer of sweet dreams,
    Each word costing a year of my life.

I bend on joints,
    Ancient and stiff,
    To kiss their dear heads.

Then I begin the journey back to my solace,
    And yearn for the day I no longer move.

Reset.

Sometimes you need to turn off your system and then back on;
   It is the first solution proposed when anything stops functioning,
   so why would the same not work for your brain?

Maybe this time of powering down has now enabled me to return to operating smoothly.
   But to ensure I do not crash again I need to not push myself beyond my boundaries.

Feeling.

I
   Hate
   Feeling.

It makes me uncomfortable.
   Why are we conditioned to run from what we feel?

If I never allow myself to feel my emotions they will take me hostage,
   Drowning me in their weight.

Oceans.

Wave after wave the emotions come.

Some days it storms,
    They crash against my heart in violent swells stealing my breath.

Some days the pool is calm,
    Gentle ripples soothe my restless soul.

I have no control over how they come,
    So I brace myself against the rocks with a watchful eye.
    Feeling hurts.

Tipping Scales.

How do you weight pain against pleasure?

So often I wish to feel nothing at all.
   Life pushes and challenges you with trials and pain
   Making you wish to push it all away.

But if you numb yourself what do you lose?
   The beauty of a sunrise,
   The giggle of a child,
   The kiss of one you love.

What weighs more?
   Despair or Hope.

If you turn off your heart will you regret the loss,
   Or find peace in the nothing?

Identity.

Do you know who you are?
　　Or have you lost yourself in pursuit of who you should be?

Everyday someone or something carves away a piece of my existence.
　　I am told this piece is no good,
　　　So I pick up the shard and tuck it away.

They weld their thoughts into my mind,
　　Am I even me?

Can I reassemble the shards of my true self?
　　Can I pick up the pieces from the hidden box deep within and bring them into the light?

Will mending my broken soul let me move forward in joy and love;
　　Or will the shards cut through the remnants that linger leaving me with nothing?

Busy.

Too busy.

Too busy to think.
    Too busy to feel.
    Too busy to assess if who I am is real.

Too busy to love.
    Too busy to cry.
    Too busy to ask if this is all I want before I die.

Is too busy avoidable?
    Could I slow down?
    If I did would I find a life of joy,
    or would I be swept along in the current until I give up and drown?

Anger.

Anger rarely walks alone.

She is a mother protecting the scared emotion beside her.
   She roars at those who draw near to keep them from seeing your pain,
   Your sadness,
   Your fear or anxiety.

Anger is glorious in her strength,
   Shouldering the weight of the emotions you cannot face.
   But she grows tired of driving everyone away.

Someday Anger will collapse,
   Will you be ready to face what lies beneath?

Failure.

Failure is the cuss word we are all taught to fear.
 At no point can you allow yourself to slip into this darkest of sins.

Push yourself just a little bit harder,
 Your family says.

Push yourself just a little bit harder,
 Your colleagues say.

Push yourself just a little bit harder,
 You tell yourself.

Push yourself just a little bit harder,
 The cliff is waiting for you with an accepting smile.

Push.

Endlessly I pushed myself forward,
   Always striving for more.
   More success.
   More experience.
   More approval.

Driven each day by the need to prove that I could.
   Driven to show family I was better than the box they put me in.
   Driven to show leaders they underestimated my abilities.
   Driven to show the world I am worth their acceptance.

Driven to the point of losing my peace.
   Driven to lose my joy in life.
   Driven until I lost every last drop of my drive.

Rest.

Lord in you my soul can finally rest.
   I give you the shards of my broken life.

Take away the sharp edges that continuously cut through my peace.
   Meld them and form them into something new.

I have no more blood to bleed.
   I have no more tears to cry.
   I need your strength to stand again.

Hidden.

How much of my life have I locked away?
   How many moments are hidden from view?

I keep them tied down deep in the dark,
   Never stopping to pull them out.

How much of my soul have I locked off,
   To keep moving forward with a smile?

My existence has become so small in the remaining space.
   There is no room to think.
   There is no room to feel.

How long before light hits the dark?
   Can I face what it hides?

Confused.

My life is perfect.

My world looks so ideal.

I have it all.

So why do I not want to be me?

Judging.

The voices around me judge me.
 They peer through the lens of their existence and weigh my life.

I hear them whisper,
 I am falling short.
 I know they observe my every fault.

Daily I hide from their looming verdict.

The voices shout I am not enough.
 The voices say I do not deserve to be here.

The voices are my own.
 I am my worst critic.
 Can I shut my voices out?

Roaming.

I knew what I was supposed to be.
   I knew what I was supposed to do.

I walked the path laid before me,
   And lost myself in who they told me to be.

Now I roam this path alone,
   Unsure of what to do.

Why, if I did it all right, am I still so lost?

Cycle.

Sometimes life shocks me with its endless cycle of change.
 Every time I get settled into my existence it tilts and shifts into something new.

Some days it excites me with the continuous thrill of discovery.
 Some days I just want off this crazy ride.

Release.

Why are only certain feelings tolerated?
   Why is it applauded when we smile or laugh at histories of our lives,
   Yet we are not allowed to cry over old sorrows?

Why am I told to get over my pain,
   While my joy is celebrated whether a minute or a decade old?

I am not only capable of light,
   My darkness needs released as well or it will consume me.

Staircase.

Down the spiraling staircase I descend,
   Ever downward without end.

I spent so many years clawing my way out.
   I thought I broke each step behind me,
   Building a wall of the crumbled cement,
   Eradicating any chance of further decent.

Little did I know that life trailed behind,
   Breaking down the strongholds,
   Turning my walls into slides.

Then it lept before me unexpectedly and with one shove
   Slid me back down into the breach.

Down I slid,
   Faster than before,
   Until I came to realize what I thought was the basement was merely the ground floor.

Staircase.

The path up is now too slick,
    For me to pursue,
    So down I must creep
    To see what lies beneath.

Will I find a rope to climb,
    Or a window of escape?
    Or do these stairs end,
    Only in my grave?

Aspirations.

How did I go from dreaming to drowning so quickly?
  Moments ago I loved my path and aspirations.
  Moments ago I was happy.
  And now all I want is to run away.

I want to escape my life and just exist,
  Far away,
  Somewhere free.

I don't think I can go back.
  I don't think I can be who I need to be.

I am terrified that I have forever lost me.

So Close.

Why do I always raise the bar just far enough to ensure I fail?

Every day I grow stronger.
   Every day I achieve more.
   But for each inch I gain,
   I move the finish line two more.

I achieve my goals moments after I push them further away.
   Why can't I allow myself to feel success?

Forgiven.

If you want to forgive yourself
   You already have.

Forgiveness does not wash away regret.
   Forgiveness does not erase the pain.

Acknowledgment is the first ingredient in the balm made to heal your self-inflicted wounds.

Acceptance is a war won through a multitude of small battles.

Go easy on yourself as you fight to find your way.

Inches.

Healing comes in inches,
   And slowly creeps through your core.

One day you brace yourself,
   Only to discover the pain of remembrance doesn't follow the memory.

One more scar has formed.
   One more nerve has deadened.
   How long before all of me is numb?

Dreams.

When did I forget how to dream?

Once upon a time I had passions.
   Once upon a time I had aspirations;
   For love,
   Creativity,
   Freedom.

Somewhere along the way
   I lost my way.

There must have been a time they faded away.
   Did it take an hour, a week, a year?
   Or did it take but a second of pain for my dreams to disappear?

Inner Child.

What did you need to hear as a child that you didn't?

You are enough.
    You are loved.
    You are loved when you fail just as much as when you succeed.
    You are whole, even when you feel broken.
    You are strong, even when the weight of this life feels crushing.
    You are perfect in all your imperfections.

You are you.
    And that is all you must be.

III

Living.

A new day can be full of wonder, or it can be full of pain. Fear of the unknown can stop us from moving forward; but move on we must. Accepting what is and learning to live a life with a new reality, a new mental state is difficult but not impossible.

Cyclothymia.

Nothing stays the same.

When I am high I swear I can touch the sky.
  I fly on wings of joy and elation,
    Chasing each adventure with the thrill of childlike enthusiasm.

Most days I am unstoppable.

Until I stop.

I stop and am lost in the comfort of the floor.
  I drown in the deep of my own darkness,
    Wishing for nothing more than blissful oblivion.

Nothing stays the same.

Re-Write

Only in breaking down do I see how far I have strayed.

For so long I have chased after an unknown dream.
   Running fast without any goal.

How did I never realize I was building an empire I didn't want to rule?
   I ran as fast and hard as I could,
   Until my mind refused to move.

And in the pause that followed I finally saw the truth.
   My life is brilliant,
   And I cannot wait to re-write my story.

Masks.

How many masks do we each own?
   One for our family,
   One for our friends,
   One for our colleagues,
   Another for going out,
   One for staying in.

We mask our faces,
   We mask our emotions,
   We mask what we hold dear,
   We mask what we fear.

Do any of us truly know one another beyond mask deep?
   If I remove mine will you let yours slip?
   If only for a moment, letting our true selves meet.

Stop.

~~~~~~~~~~~

Stop trying.

You run so fast to prove yourself,
  Each moment pushing towards the unseen goal.
  Stretching yourself beyond your limits in hopes you can achieve acceptance.
  You strive for approval.

You stretch yourself,
  Dreaming of the day you will feel that others have judged you and found you sufficient.

But what if you stop?
  What if you looked within rather than without?
  What if you judged yourself to be enough?
  What if you accepted that you are truly and fully created as you are by the Maker of the universe?

If He found you worthy of His time does anyone else's opinion matter?

Pause.

Pause.
　Breathe.
　Let it go.

The weight of your existence is not yours to carry alone.
　Throw the pain into the wind.
　Drop the anger beside a stream.
　Walk in the sand and let the anxiety flow out of you into the space between the grains.

Pause.
　Breathe.
　Move forward.

Worthy.

Your worth is not measured by what you achieve.
    You will never do enough.
    You will never learn enough.
    You will never be able to achieve your way to acceptance.

You are enough and you are worthy.
    Worthy of love.
    Worthy of peace.
    Worthy of fully embracing who and what you are.

Acceptance.

Acceptance is terrifying.
   If I accept it the reality becomes real.

I don't want to face it.
   I don't want to feel it.
   I am not strong enough to accept my life.

And yet reality is real,
   Whether I wish to face it or not.

Only in acceptance can one begin to change and move forward.
   Acceptance is the freedom I need to live.

www.ingramcontent.com/pod-product-compliance
Lightning Source LLC
Chambersburg PA
CBHW051349040426
42453CB00007B/492